The Little Angel Books Series

D1739654

When the Earth Was New

An Experience in Healing Our Planet

Written & Illustrated
by Leia A. Stinnett

ISBN 0-929385-91-8

Published by

StarChild Press
a division of
Light Technology
Publishing
P.O. Box 1526
Sedona, Arizona 86339
(520) 282-6523

Printed by

**MISSION
POSSIBLE
Commercial
Printing**

P.O. Box 1495
Sedona, AZ

When the Earth Was New
An Experience in Healing Our Planet

Written & Illustrated
by Leia A. Stinnett

A Special Introduction . . .

Boys and girls . . .
I would like to introduce
you to Anya.
You will like Anya. She
has a very special interest
in children because, you see,
Anya is a child herself . . .
a child of God . . . a little angel.

And just like you, Anya has
come to Earth to bring light,
love and laughter to our planet
and to all the wondrous
creatures of nature who make
Earth their home.

Anya comes to present
to you wonderful stories,
meditations and exercises that

you can work with at home.

Through these lessons you will better understand just how special you really are, how you can help make the world a much happier place in which to live, and how you can create for yourself a better life, while at the same time helping to create a more joyful, peaceful, and loving Earth . . . for all people.

Anya has many stories to share with you, my special friends. She hopes you will enjoy these stories and have fun learning all about yourselves and your Earth by reading the lessons and doing the special meditations and exercises she has created . . . just for you!

Anya's Special Report to Earth's Children

My name is Anya. I have traveled to Earth at this very important time in history to help you and other people understand the wonderful, positive changes that are taking place on this great planet right now.

I am happy to report that mankind is finally giving some serious thought to the condition of our Earth, and is making plans to conserve our natural resources and protect our Earth's environment from any more damage.

People all over the world are joining together to work on improving conditions on Earth . . . and, very slowly, they are making progress.

It is never too late to make changes for the better in anything we do. And it certainly is not too late to save the beautiful Earth if we begin now and work together.

Children of Earth, I know you are as concerned as I am about the precious Earth.

I know you are sad about the animals being destroyed, about the Earth's ozone layer being eaten away from toxins released into the air by careless people.

I know you are sad to see Earth's beautiful lakes and

waterways and her majestic
oceans polluted with garbage
and chemicals.

And I especially know how
unhappy you are with the
cutting down of the rainforests
of the world.

I am sure you realize that

these great forests help make the oxygen you breathe, and that by cutting down the trees, mankind is decreasing his own supply of what he needs to live on Earth.

I am here now to tell you about the Earth when it was very different from what you see today. My story will help you see just how much the Earth has changed since mankind arrived.

Then I will share with you my very favorite Earth healing meditation. You can use this meditation any time you feel like sending the Earth some love and healing energy.

Close your eyes as I take you now on a journey into our Earth's past.

Take a deep breath and
follow along with your
imagination as we travel back
in time to when the Earth was
new, lush with fresh plant
and animal life, glowing in
good health.

In your mind imagine the
Earth without cities, freeways
and factories. Picture the Earth
now covered with tall green
trees . . . lots of trees – tall trees
and short trees, trees reaching
high into the sky, toward the
light.

Imagine all the beautiful flowering plants covering the land. Smell the fragrant flowers. Even with your eyes closed you can feel the healing energy of the color green radiating from the leaves of the trees and plants around you.

Look down at your feet. Look down at the Earth. Imagine that your feet are now part of the deep, rich soil as it waits for one tiny seed to land on its surface so it can wrap the tiny seed securely in its arms, nurturing and loving it until it becomes a beautiful, full-grown plant or tree.

In your imagination, add to your picture many brilliant-colored, lively birds singing happy songs, and colorful butterflies flitting about the flowers.

Imagine all your favorite animals, playfully dancing in the forest of trees and flowers, all enjoying the beauty of nature around them.

What you are seeing now is a picture of how nature lives in harmony with all living things. Each plant, animal, rock, tree and body of water, even the soil, respects the space and importance of the other living things.

Each part of nature, each living creature, takes only what it needs to survive.

By taking only what each needs to survive - nothing more - all of Earth's living things share equally in the joyful task of keeping Earth in balance.

Now imagine fresh, cool streams, rivers and lakes on the Earth. Imagine each body of water free from discarded paper, tin cans, toxic waste, bottles, old tires and sewage.

See the fish and water life swimming briskly in the clear, fresh water. Listen to the sounds of the water as it rushes

over the rocks in its path. It
seems to sing a song of joy.

Listen carefully!
Shhhhhhh! What song does
the water sing to you?

Look out now over the
deep blue ocean and see the
ocean free of sticky black oil
from spills that have occurred
over and over when ships
carrying the oil were damaged
at sea.

See the ocean clear of the
toxic waste containers and
other pollutants and watch as
the sea birds dance in the air,
dipping quickly into the
surface of the water, snatching
up their dinner.

If you are very quiet, you
will hear the songs of the
whales and dolphins playfully

calling you . . . "Come, play with me. Come, hear my song of love."

This is the picture, children, of Earth when the Earth was new.

What is missing from this picture?

You have seen the plants, the trees, the animals, the clean, clear air and water. You have seen the rich, fertile soil.

You have seen the Earth when it was new. What is missing from your picture?

Yes. You are right. People are missing from your picture.

When humans first came to Earth, they took only what they needed to survive. They had great respect for nature. Humankind and nature lived together in what we call harmony . . . a feeling of peaceful sharing and caring for one another, a feeling where everyone loves one another, where there is no arguing or conflict.

Humans cut down only those trees they needed to build a comfortable home. They cleared only the plant life necessary to make a space for a garden or a field in which to plant food crops.

They killed only those

animals they needed for food and clothing.

They respected the clear lakes and streams, realizing that it was this water that helped them stay alive.

This was a time on Earth when all was well in the world. All was in balance on the planet.

All living things — the plants, animals, rocks and human beings — worked toward one common goal: keeping a cycle of balance and sharing in the Earth's riches.

All lived together in harmony with each other, in harmony with the entire universe. All was well in the world and in the universe.

Then a very sad time came to Earth and to all her living

creatures, plants, trees and flowers. There came a time when people stopped taking only what they needed to survive. They became greedy and self-centered, wanting more and more "things" . . . lots of things.

In order to get all they wanted, they cut down the beautiful forests to make room for cities and freeways. They built dams to create the power needed to operate the cities and different types of machinery.

In the process people changed the flow of the lakes and rivers, leaving many of Earth's creatures without a home.

Humans began to build

more and more types of
machinery and automobiles,
giving little thought to what
these pieces of metal, rubber
and whatnot might do to the
environment, to the Earth.

They began to hunt
animals for the sport of killing,

taking their tusks and heads
for trophies, selling their furs to
make exquisite coats for those
who could afford to
purchase them.
   People created
wastelands in the path of
what they called
progress. And in this
path they brought
destruction
and hardship
to all life along
the way.

Humans began to pull further and further away from their spiritual nature, becoming more materialistic, more fascinated with their own power. How much could they take for themselves, even if they had to take away from all the others?

No matter how much they took, it was never enough. There never seemed to be enough to satisfy their wants.

Humans' greed has caused the Earth and her creatures much pain. Humans feel they are dominant over the world of nature. That is, they feel they are in charge over, and more powerful than, the animals, plants, rocks, water.

But are humans really in

charge? Stop and think about it for a moment.

Isn't it true that all of nature can survive without people?

Yes, but can humans survive without nature?

Can people survive without the plants and animals for food and clothing?

Can they survive without the trees which provide oxygen for the air they breathe and material for building homes?

Can humans survive without the rich soil in which to plant and nurture their crops?

Can people survive if all the water and air of the world is polluted?

Certainly Not!

Yes, children, this is indeed a very sad story.

But, wait! There is a happy ending. Want to hear what it is?

Each of us has the power within us to change this picture of destruction. We are all children of God, part of God. By using God's loving, positive, creative energy in our thoughts, we can heal our planet. As we put our loving energy out into the world, we also touch the hearts of all people everywhere.

They, too, will turn from their paths of destruction and want to help create a new, beautiful world of peace, love and harmony . . . a place where each of us will be proud to live and call home.

I will now show you how to use your creative power, your creative energy, your imagination, to heal the Earth.

Sit quietly on the floor or in a chair with your spine very straight.

This will help the energy flow smoothly and freely in your body, helping you to relax.

Begin to breathe very deeply as you let your body relax more and more.

Place your hands, palms up, on your thighs as you continue to relax your body.

Imagine God's white light coming down through the top of your head and down into your arms and hands. You will begin to sense a warmth in your hands as you concentrate on bringing God's light into your body.

Now reach your arms up over your head and place your flat palms together, making a circle around your head.

Concentrate on the inside

of this circle. Imagine a golden
light of healing energy glowing
brighter and brighter,
beginning to fill this entire
space.

Soon you will feel this
warm, glowing energy filling
the space within the circle you
have just made using your arms
and hands. You will feel this
energy becoming stronger
and stronger.

As you open your hands,
imagine this healing energy
floating up and out into the air.

With your mind, direct the
energy to flow into the air,
the atmosphere, the animals,
lakes, streams, rivers and
oceans, the plants and trees,
the rocks and soil . . . and to
all the people of Earth . . .

touching the entire planet . . .
all of nature.

See the Earth glow in a
golden light as the healing
begins to take place. Create a
picture of the Earth in your
mind, a picture like the one we
made earlier when the Earth
was new. Imagine healthy
green trees and plants.

Imagine fresh, clean water
in all the oceans, lakes, rivers
and streams.

Imagine rich, fertile soil
free of pollutants. Imagine
plentiful animal life everywhere
in the world.

Then imagine a picture of
humankind. From your heart
send a pink ray of love out to
all the people of Earth.

See them smiling as they

receive your love, releasing
their feelings of fear and of not
caring for the Earth . . . now
feeling only LOVE for their
home planet.

Remember,

LOVE is the most powerful
emotion in our universe.
Where there is love, there is no
darkness, no negative or
destructive thoughts, feelings
or ideas.

Love can change our fears,
worries, our anger. The more
love we send out to all living
things, all over the world, the
more healing we help create on
this planet . . . and within
ourselves.

When we give out love, love
is returned to us many times,
and we are healed in the process.

Open your eyes now. You have done a wonderful job in sending healing energy out onto the Earth to all of Earth's living things.

It is important that we all work together in offering healing energy to our planet. Working as a team creates ten times more loving, healing energy than when we work by ourselves.

Thank you for sharing this time with me. You have done well with your first lesson. I look forward to returning with a new lesson for you.

In the meantime, can you think of some ways you can help take care of our Earth?

Share your ideas with your parents, with your teachers and friends.

Practice your Earth healing meditation as often as you like.

Create your own Earth healing meditation and share it with your friends and family.

Each time you send healing energy, loving healing energy, out into the world, you are taking an active role in making the Earth a better place for all of nature and God's children, where each of us can grow and learn in harmony and peace with one another. Each of us is important. Each of us can make a difference.

I love you all . . .

Anya

Here are some things you can do right now to help keep our Earth smiling:

1. **Recycle glass, plastic and aluminum.** Many cities have special recycling centers where you can collect money from recycled items taken to these centers. This is a great way to make some extra pocket money while helping the Earth.

2. **Go through your closet and storage areas.** Find old clothing and toys which can be taken to special thrift stores or swap meets. Have you ever heard the old saying, "One man's junk is

another man's treasure"?
You might be surprised at
the number of people who
want your old toy truck or
doll. So, pass it on.

3. **Don't use styrofoam
   products.** Styrofoam does
   not dissolve back into the
   Earth. If you were to bury a
   piece of styrofoam in your
   backyard, today, ten years
   from now, twenty years from
   now, even fifty years from
   now or longer it will still be
   right where you buried it.
   Encourage others not to buy
   styrofoam products as well.

4. **Use cloth towels instead
   of paper towels to wipe**

your hands.

5. **Reuse your aluminum foil, plastic or paper bags.**

6. **Make a habit of picking up after yourself** whenever you are camping, visiting the beach, forest or lakes. You can make a special project out of cleaning up a favorite area of nature. Many organizations now adopt a section of highway to help keep the Earth beautiful. Whether you belong to a club or just gather a group of friends, you can do this too.

7. **Encourage your parents to repair leaky faucets, showers, toilets and other plumbing**. A tiny leak can

cost millions of gallons of water over a short period of time.

8. **If you are unable to finish drinking your glass of water, don't throw it down the drain.** Water your lawn, plants, trees, flowers, or even your pets. Don't waste this valuable resource.

9. **Plant a tree to help the forest and conserve our soil.**

10. **Save newspapers, magazines and other paper products for recycling.** Many cities have various paper recycling

locations. Check them out in your neighborhood.

11. **Help the rainforest** by not buying products that come from animals raised on land where the trees have been cut down to make room for grazing.

12. **Buy a living Christmas tree.**

13. **Purchase rechargeable batteries.**

14. **Be a light monitor at home.** Help remind other members of your family to turn out lights they are not using.

15. **Encourage family members to walk more and leave the**

family car in the garage.
Not only will you all get
some great exercise and see
some beautiful scenery you
may not have noticed
before, but you will be
helping to minimize air
pollution.

16. **Keep the refrigerator door
closed.** Don't hold the
door open for a long
period of time trying to
choose something to eat.
Think about what you
want before you open the
refrigerator door.

17. **Start a recycling program
at your school.** Get your
friends involved.

18. Keep sending the Earth love — LOTS OF LOVE.

Write down some ways you can help our Earth:

1. _____
   _____

2. _____
   _____

3. _____
   _____

4. _____
   _____

5. _____
   _____

6. _____
   _____

7. _____

_____

8. _____

_____

9. _____

_____

10. _____

_____

11. _____

_____

12. _____

_____

When the Earth Was New
Coloring Pages!

Other Books by Leia Stinnett:

A Circle of Angels
The Twelve Universal Laws

The Little Angel Books Series:
The Angel Told Me to Tell You Good-bye
The Bridge Between Two Worlds
Color Me One
Crystals R for Kids
Exploring the Chakras
One Red Rose
Where Is God?
Who's Afraid of the Dark?

All My Angel Friends (Coloring Book)

About the Author

The '80s were a decade of self-discovery for Leia Stinnett after she began researching many different avenues of spirituality. In her profession as a graphic designer she had become restless, knowing there was something important she had to do outside the materiality of corporate America. In August 1986 Leia had her first contact with Archangel Michael when he appeared in a physical form of glowing blue light. A voice said, "I am Michael. Together we will save the children."

In 1988 she was inspired by Michael to teach spiritual classes in Sacramento, California, the Circle of Angels. Through these classes she had the opportunity to work with learning-disabled children, children of abuse and those from dysfunctional homes.

Later Michael told her, "Together we are going to write the Little Angel Books." To date Leia and Michael have created thirteen Little Angel Books that present various topics of spiritual truths and principles. The books proved popular among adults as well as children.

The Circle of Angels classes have been introduced to several countries around the world and across the U.S., and Leia and her husband Douglas now have a teacher's manual and training program for people who wish to offer spiritual classes to children. Leia and Michael have been interviewed on Canadian Satellite TV and have appeared on NBC-TV's *Angels II – Beyond the Light,* which featured their Circle of Angels class and discussed their books and Michael's visit.

The angels have given Leia and Douglas a vision of a new educational system without competition or grades — one that supports love and positive self-esteem, honoring all children as the independent lights they are. Thus they are now writing a curriculum for the new "schools of light" and developing additional books and programs for children.